The Universe

Words by Larry A. Ciupik

Associate Astronomer and Doane Observatory Director
The Adler Planetarium

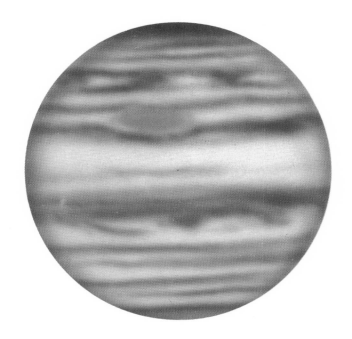

Raintree Childrens Books
Milwaukee • Toronto • Melbourne • London

Library of Congress Number: 77-27567

6 7 8 9 0 85 84 83

Printed and bound in the United States of America.

Library of Congress Cataloging in Publication Data

Ciupik, Larry A.
  The universe.

  (Read about)
  Bibliography: p.
  Includes index.
  SUMMARY: Discusses the various planets, moons,
constellations, solar systems, and galaxies that
make up the universe and some of the instruments
used to explore it.
  1. Astronomy—Juvenile literature. [1. As-
tronomy] I. Title.
QB46.M855   520   77-27567
ISBN 0-8393-0089-1 lib. bdg.

The Universe

sun

stars

If you watch the sun for a long time, it seems to move across the sky from east to west. For hundreds of years people thought that the sun moved around the earth. Now we know it is the earth that moves around the sun.

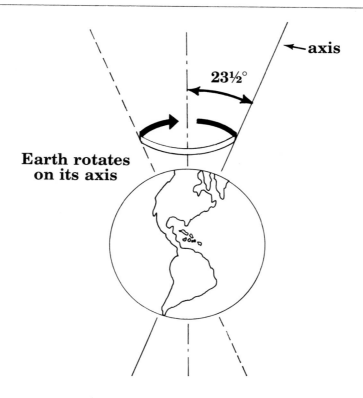

axis

23½°

Earth rotates
on its axis

You may think that you are standing still, but you are moving. This is because the ground you are standing on is moving. The earth turns. This is called the earth's rotation. It takes one day for the earth to turn all the way around. When our part of the earth faces the sun, it is day. When the earth turns away from the sun, it is night. At night we can see the moon and stars.

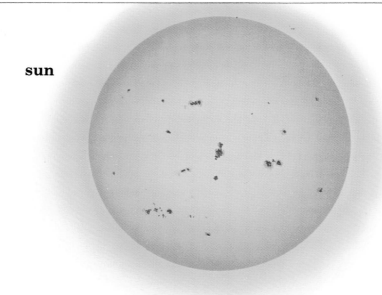

sun

Stars are giant balls of burning gas. Stars give off their own heat and light. The sun is a star. It is about the same size as most other stars. The sun looks much bigger and brighter than other stars. That is because it is much closer to us. The earth gets all of its heat and almost all of its light from the sun.

Some places on the sun are not as hot as others. Cooler places look like dark spots. They are called sunspots. In other places great flames sometimes leap from the sun. They are very hot.

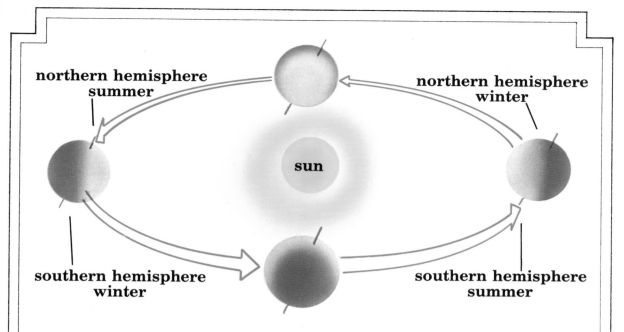

northern hemisphere
summer

northern hemisphere
winter

sun

southern hemisphere
winter

southern hemisphere
summer

    As the earth rotates, it moves around the sun. This movement is called revolving. The path around the sun is called an orbit. It takes the earth one year to revolve all the way around the sun.

    The earth tilts a little to one side. For part of the year the top half of the earth (northern hemisphere) tilts toward the sun. When this happens, it is summer there. When the top of the earth is tilted away from the sun, it is winter there. When it is summer in one hemisphere it is winter in the other.

near side

far side

The moon is called a satellite of the earth. This is because it orbits the earth. Like all satellites the moon reflects the light of a star. The moon gets light from the sun. It sends the light back out into space.

The same side of the moon always faces the earth. This is called the near side. We cannot see the far side of the moon from earth. Astronauts went to the moon in spaceships. They took pictures of both sides. They also brought back rocks.

crater

The moon takes about one month to revolve once around the earth. As the moon revolves, it rotates very slowly. Once a month all of the near side is bright. This is called a full moon. Once a month all of the near side is dark. This is called a new moon.

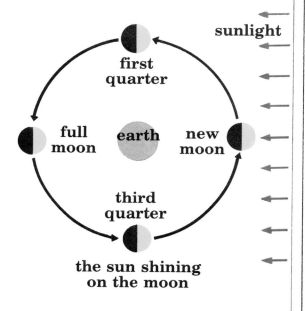

sunlight

first quarter

full moon

earth

new moon

third quarter

the sun shining on the moon

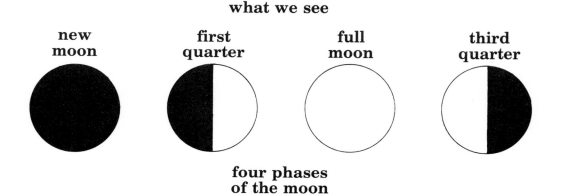

what we see

new moon

first quarter

full moon

third quarter

four phases of the moon

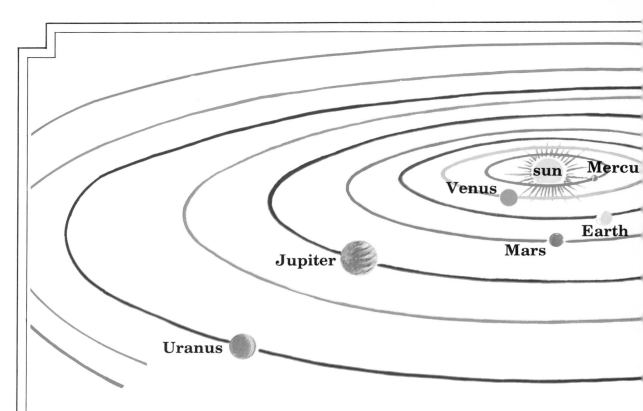

The earth is a satellite of the sun. It reflects the sun's light. Nine satellites of the sun have a special name. They are called planets. The earth is a planet. The sun and its planets and their satellites are called the solar system. Solar means "belonging to the sun."

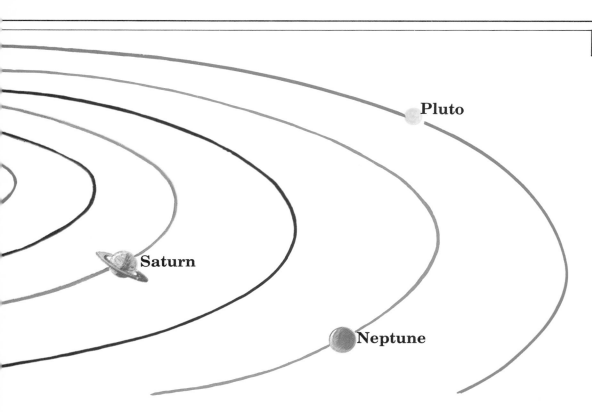

Some planets have orbits that are smaller than the earth's. It takes them less than a year to go around the sun. They are hotter than the earth because they are closer to the sun.

Other planets have orbits that are larger than the earth's. It takes them more than a year to go around the sun. They are cooler than the earth because they are farther away from the sun.

Mercury

Mercury is the closest planet to the sun. It has only hot, dry land. Nothing lives there.

Venus is the second planet from the sun. It is the closest planet to the earth. Thick clouds cover Venus. The clouds keep in the heat. This makes the surface of Venus very hot. Photographs of Venus show rocky, sandy places.

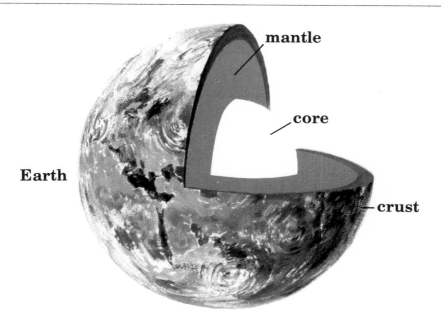

Earth

mantle

core

crust

Earth is the third planet from the sun. The earth has different parts or layers. The top layer is the crust. It is about a mile thick. The next layer is the mantle. It is made up of rocks. The mantle is hotter than the crust. The middle of the earth is the core. It is partly liquid and partly solid. The core is the hottest part of the earth.

There are gases around the earth. They make up the earth's atmosphere. We usually call this the air. We need these gases to live on the earth.

Mars

Mars is the fourth planet from the sun. Long ago, people saw long, straight lines on Mars. The lines looked like canals. Today we know that they are not canals. The lines are groups of craters that look like canals from far away.

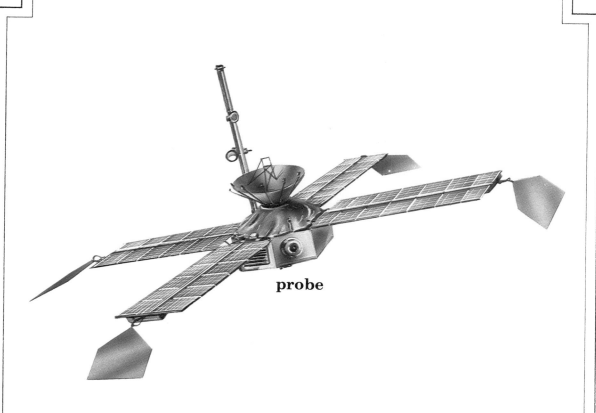

probe

   A special kind of spaceship called a
probe took pictures of Mars. Mars looks like
a rocky desert in the pictures.

Jupiter

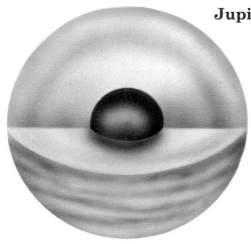

solid center
or
mostly liquid

The fifth planet from the sun is Jupiter. It is called the giant planet because it is the biggest. Jupiter has at least 14 moons. Some of them are bigger than our moon. Some are only a few miles wide. Gases cover all of Jupiter. Inside, it might be gas too. It might be solid inside. No one knows for sure.

Between Mars and Jupiter, there are asteroids. Asteroids are pieces of rock that orbit the sun. Asteroids are much smaller than the planets. Ceres is the biggest asteroid. It is about the size of Great Britain.

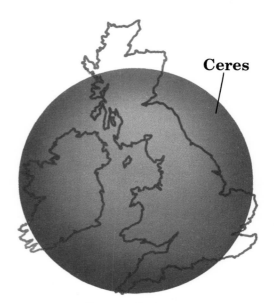

Ceres

Great Britain

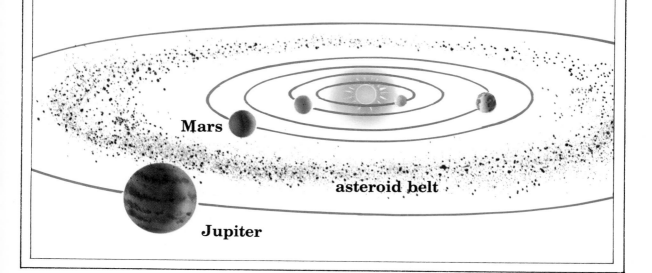

Mars

asteroid belt

Jupiter

The sixth planet from the sun is Saturn. It is the second largest planet. It has at least 10 moons. Saturn also has small pieces of rock and ice circling around it. When the sun shines on these moving pieces, they look like rings. The rings make Saturn look very beautiful.

The last three planets in the solar system are Uranus, Neptune, and Pluto. They are very cold because they are far from the sun.

Uranus and Neptune are large planets. They look green because part of their atmosphere is a green gas. The gas is called methane. It is poisonous to humans.

Pluto is the farthest planet from the sun. It takes Pluto about 248 years to orbit the sun one time. It is always very cold on Pluto.

Uranus

Neptune

Pluto

Milky Way

On a clear night, we can see a thick band of light in the sky. This band is a giant group of stars called a galaxy. This galaxy is named the Milky Way. Our solar system is only a tiny part of the Milky Way.

**Milky Way
side view**

The Milky Way looks long and thin to us because we are part of it. It would look very different if we could see it from the top. Then we would see its curved shape. This shape is called a spiral.

**Milky Way
top view**

The Milky Way is only one galaxy. There are many, many others. All the stars in the universe are in one galaxy or another. Many of these stars are so far away that we cannot see them when we look at the sky.

Galaxies have different shapes. Here are two different shapes.

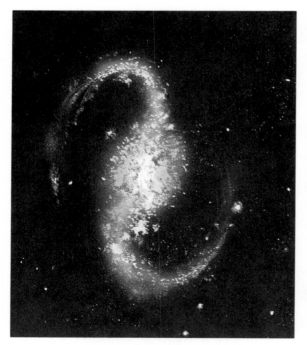

barred spiral

irregular

comet

meteor

Sometimes we can see bright streaks of light moving in the night sky. These streaks are comets and meteors.

A comet is a large lump of ice and dust. The sun warms the ice and turns it into gas. The gas glows. The pieces of dust reflect light from the sun. These give the comet its fiery-looking tail.

A meteor is a small piece of rock and metal that circles the sun. When a meteor comes too close to the earth, it burns up in the air. When this happens, it makes a bright streak of light. A meteor is also called a shooting star. Sometimes part of a meteor reaches earth. This part is called a meteorite.

radio telescope

Today astronomers can find out about stars and galaxies that cannot be seen at all. They use special telescopes. One of these is called a radio telescope.

Galaxies send out light in waves. They also send out special waves called radio waves. The radio telescope picks up these waves. Astronomers make pictures from these waves. This helps us to learn more about a galaxy.

observatory

Stars and planets are very far away. We cannot see them very well. An observatory is a place that has a big telescope. Telescopes help us see stars and planets better. Telescopes can also be used to take pictures of objects that are very far away. Astronomers are scientists who use telescopes to learn about the universe.

telescope

All of us look at the sky and stars. Many times we do not really understand what we are looking at. A planetarium can help us learn about what we see every day.

A planetarium is a special kind of theater. It has a large ceiling that is shaped like a bowl turned upside down. Moving pictures of the sun, moon, planets, and stars are shown on the ceiling of a planetarium.

planetarium

Long ago, people pretended that groups of stars made pictures in the sky. We still use this idea today. We call these groups constellations.

Each constellation is named for the picture it makes. One constellation is called Orion. He was a famous hunter in mythology.

Orion

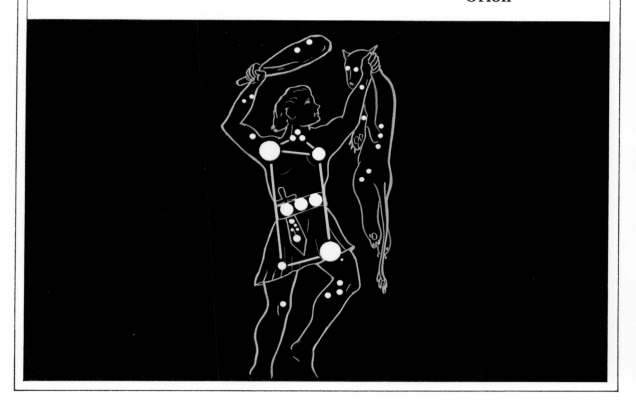

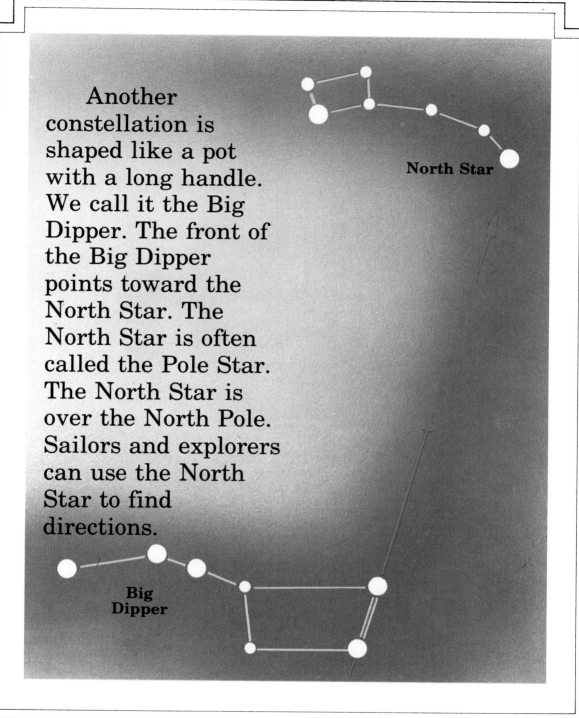

Another constellation is shaped like a pot with a long handle. We call it the Big Dipper. The front of the Big Dipper points toward the North Star. The North Star is often called the Pole Star. The North Star is over the North Pole. Sailors and explorers can use the North Star to find directions.

North Star

Big Dipper

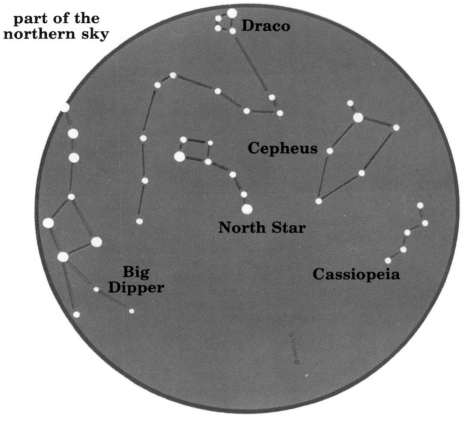

part of the northern sky

Draco

Cepheus

North Star

Big Dipper

Cassiopeia

Different constellations can be seen from different parts of the earth. This is because the northern hemisphere and the southern hemisphere face different parts of the sky. A person living in the northern hemisphere sees one group of constellations. Someone living in the southern hemisphere sees a different group of constellations.

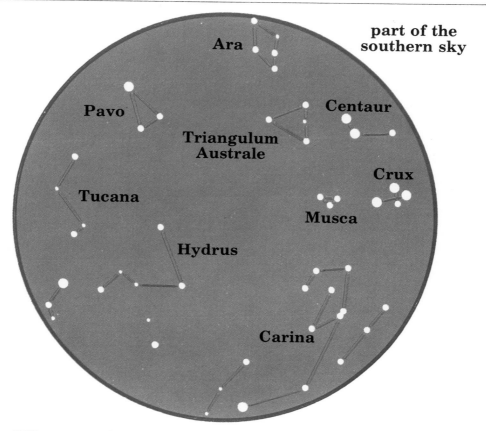

We see different constellations as the
earth moves around the sun. In December
we see constellations that are different from
those we see in June.

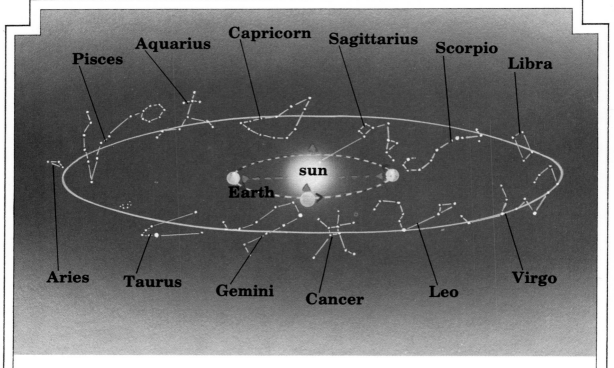

There are 12 special constellations called the zodiac. The zodiac forms a circle around the sun. As the earth follows its orbit, different constellations of the zodiac can be seen.

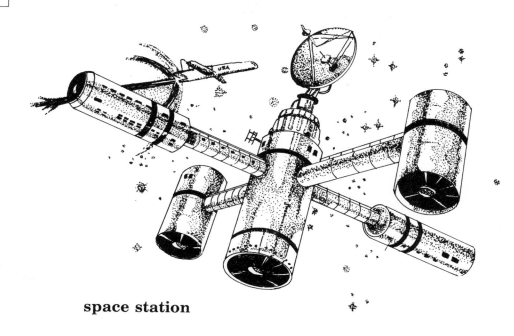

space station

People have already left the earth and traveled into space. Our spaceships fly among the planets. We have even walked on the moon.

Scientists are trying to find ways for people to live in space. Maybe someday we could live on a space station like this one.

The Metric System

In the United States, things are measured in inches, pounds, quarts, and so on. Most countries of the world use centimeters, kilograms, and liters for these things. The United States uses the American system to measure things. Most other countries use the metric system. By 1985, the United States will be using the metric system, too.

In some books, you will see two systems of measurement. For example, you might see a sentence like this: "That bicycle wheel is 27 inches (69 centimeters) across." When all countries have changed to the metric system, inches will not be used any more. But until then, you may sometimes have to change measurements from one system to the other. The chart on the next page will help you.

All you have to do is multiply the unit of measurement in Column 1 by the number in Column 2. That gives you the unit in Column 3.

Suppose you want to change 5 inches to centimeters. First, find inches in Column 1. Next, multiply 5 times 2.54. You get 12.7. So, 5 inches is 12.7 centimeters.

Column 1	Column 2	Column 3
THIS UNIT OF MEASUREMENT	**TIMES THIS NUMBER**	**GIVES THIS UNIT OF MEASUREMENT**
inches	2.54	centimeters
feet	30.	centimeters
feet	.3	meters
yards	.9	meters
miles	1.6	kilometers
ounces	28.	grams
pounds	.45	kilograms
fluid ounces	.03	liters
pints	.47	liters
quarts	.95	liters
gallons	3.8	liters
centimeters	.4	inches
meters	1.1	yards
kilometers	.6	miles
grams	.035	ounces
kilograms	2.2	pounds
liters	33.8	fluid ounces
liters	2.1	pints
liters	1.06	quarts
liters	.26	gallons

Where to Read About
the Universe

Pronunciation Key

a	a as in **cat, bad**
ā	a as in **able**, ai as in **train**, ay as in **play**
ä	a as in **father, car**, o as in **cot**
e	e as in **bend, yet**
ē	e as in **me**, ee as in **feel**, ea as in **beat**, ie as in **piece**, y as in **heavy**
i	i as in **in, pig**, e as in **pocket**
ī	i as in **ice, time**, ie as in **tie**, y as in **my**
o	o as in **top**, a as in **watch**
ō	o as in **old**, oa as in **goat**, ow as in **slow**, oe as in **toe**
ô	o as in **cloth**, au as in **caught**, aw as in **paw**, a as in **all**
oo	oo as in **good**, u as in **put**
o͞o	oo as in **tool**, ue as in **blue**
oi	oi as in **oil**, oy as in **toy**
ou	ou as in **out**, ow as in **plow**
u	u as in **up, gun**, o as in **other**
ur	ur as in **fur**, er as in **person**, ir as in **bird**, or as in **work**
yo͞o	u as in **use**, ew as in **few**
ə	a as in **again**, e as in **broken**, i as in **pencil**, o as in **attention**, u as in **surprise**
ch	ch as in **such**
ng	ng as in **sing**
sh	sh as in **shell, wish**
th	th as in **three, bath**
t̲h̲	th as in **that, together**

GLOSSARY

These words are defined the way they are used in this book

alive (ə līv′) having life; living

area (er′ ē ə) a special region or place

asteroid (as′ tə roid′) the rocks that orbit the sun between Mars and Jupiter

astronaut (as′ trə nôt′) a person who travels in a spaceship

astronomer (əs tron′ ə mər) a person who studies and knows a lot about the stars and planets

atmosphere (at′ məs fēr′) gases that surround a planet; the air that is all around the earth

average (av′ ər ij) usual; typical

axis (ak′ sis) the imaginary line through the center of the earth around which the earth rotates

beneath (bi nēth′) to be under something else

bowl (bōl) a curved dish that holds things

canal (kə nal′) a ditch made by people, used to bring water from one place to another

cannot (kan′ ot) is not able; can not

ceiling (sē′ ling) the top of a room

center (sen′ tər) the middle of something

century (sen′ chər ē) one hundred years

cloud (kloud) a gray or white mass of water drops or bits of ice floating in the sky

comet (käm′ it) a lump of rock, ice, and gas that travels through space

completely (kəm plēt′ lē) entirely; all

constellation (kon′ stə lā′ shən) a group of stars that form a picture in the sky

core (kôr) the central part of something

crater (krā′ tər) the hole in the ground where a meteorite has hit

crust (krust) the hard, outer surface of something

curved (kurvd) being bent in one direction

desert (dez′ ərt) a place that is dry and has few or no living things

diameter (dī am′ ə tər) how wide a round thing is from one side to the other

directly (di rekt′ lē) in a straight line

east (ēst) the direction of the sun in the morning; one of the four points on a compass

exist (eg zist′) to be real

explorer (eks plôr′ ər) a person who travels to unknown places to find out about them

famous (fā′ məs) known to many people

fiery (fī′ ər ē) hot or bright; like a fire

flame (flām) the bright, light part of a fire

flare (fler) a great flame that leaps from the sun

flow (flō) to move like water

galaxy (gal′ ək sē) a huge group of stars and their satellites

gas (gas) something that is not solid or liquid

glow (glō) to shine or look bright

heat (hēt) to make something hot or warm; warmth

hemisphere (hem' is fēr') one half of the earth

huge (hyōōj) very big; giant

human (hyōō' mən) a person on earth

layer (lā' ər) one thickness of a thing

liquid (lik' wid) something that flows like water; not a gas or solid

mantle (mant' əl) the second, rocky layer of the earth

mass (mas) the amount of matter that a body contains

maximum (mak' sə məm) the highest number or amount that can be reached

metal (met' əl) a hard substance usually found in rocks, such as iron and silver

meteor (mē' tē ər) a meteoroid that is falling to earth; the bright streak of light that a falling meteoroid makes

meteorite (mē' tē ə rīt') the part of a meteor that lands on earth

meteoroid (mē′ tē ə roid′) a lump of rock and metal that travels around the sun in a long orbit

methane (meth′ ān) a green gas that is part of the atmosphere of Uranus and Neptune

moon (mo͞on) a satellite of a planet

mythology (mi thäl′ ə jē) stories that were made up to explain what people did not know or understand

northern hemisphere (nôr′ thərn hem′ is fēr′) the northern, or top, half of the earth

object (ob′ jikt) a thing; something that can be seen and touched

observatory (əb zur′ və tôr′ ē) a place or building that has one or more telescopes; a place where an astronomer can study the universe

orbit (ôr′ bit) the path that one thing follows as it circles around another thing in space

pattern (pat′ ərn) the way colors,

shapes, or objects are put in a special order

photograph (fō′ tə graf′) a picture taken by a camera

planet (plan′ it) one of the nine large satellites of the sun

planetarium (plan′ ə ter′ ē əm) a place where moving pictures of the universe are shown on a curved ceiling

poisonous (poi′ zə nəs) able to cause sickness or death when eaten, touched, or breathed

probe (prōb) a spaceship that is used to learn about the universe

radio telescope (rā′ dē ō′ tel′ ə skōp′) a special telescope that makes pictures from the radio waves of stars

radio waves (rā′ dē ō′ wāvz′) electric waves that are sent through the air or space

reflect (ri flekt′) to send or throw back

regular (reg′ yə lər) happening over and over again in the usual way

revolve (ri volv′) to move in a path around some central point or object

rotate (rō′ tāt) to turn around and around

rotation (rō tā′ shən) the act of turning around and around

sailor (sā′ lər) someone who sails a boat

satellite (sat′ əl īt′) an object that orbits another larger object

scientist (sī′ ən tist) someone who studies and knows about some branch of science

solar system (sō′ lər sis′ təm) the sun and all its satellites

solid (sol′ id) something that has a shape and is not gas or liquid

southern hemisphere (su<u>th</u>′ ərn hem′ is fēr′) the southern, or bottom, half of the earth

space (spās) the area in which the universe exists; the area beyond the earth's atmosphere

spaceship (spās′ ship′) a machine that travels in outer space

space station (spās′ stā′ shən) an
 object in space that people may be able
 to live on some day

spin (spin) to turn around and around
 quickly

spiral (spī′ rəl) a curved, winding shape,
 like a spring

streak (strēk) a thin mark or line

sunspot (sun spät) a dark, cooler place
 on the surface of the sun

surface (sur′ fis) the top or outer part of
 something

surround (sə round′) to be all around
 something; on every side

telescope (tel′ ə skōp′) an instrument
 that helps astronomers see other
 planets, moons, stars, and galaxies. A
 telescope makes faraway objects seem
 larger and nearer.

temperature (tem′ pər ə chər) the
 amount of heat or cold in something

theater (thē′ ə tər) a place where
 motion pictures or plays are shown

tilt (tilt) not straight up and down; to be slanted to one side

travel (trav′ əl) to move from one place to another

understand (un′ dər stand′) to know the meaning of; to know something very well

universe (yoo′ nə vurs′) everything that exists, including the solar system, stars, and space

upside down (up′ sīd doun′) turned so that the top of something becomes the bottom

west (west) the direction of the sun in the evening; one of the four points on a compass

zodiac (zō′ dē ak′) 12 constellations that make a circle around the sun

Bibliography

Asimov, Isaac. *To the Ends of the Universe.*
New York: Walker Publishing Co., 1976.

Branley, Franklyn M. *The Nine Planets.* New York:
Thomas Y. Crowell Co., 1971.

Gribbin, John. *Astronomy for the Amateur.*
New York: David McKay Co., Inc., 1977.

Leonard, Jonathan N., and Sagan, Carl. *Planets.*
Morristown, N.J.: Silver Burdett Co., 1969.

Lyon, Jene. *Astronomy: Our Sun and Its Neighbors.*
Racine, Wis.: Western Publishing Co., 1974.

Nourse, Alan E. *The Backyard Astronomer.*
New York: Franklin Watts, 1973.

Peltier, Leslie C. *Guideposts to the Stars: Exploring
the Skies Throughout the Year.* New York:
Macmillan Inc., 1972.

Simak, Clifford D. *Wonder and Glory: The Story of
the Universe.* New York: St. Martin's Press, 1970.

Whitney, Charles A. *Discovery of Our Galaxy.*
New York: Alfred A. Knopf, Inc., 1971.